Scrumptious Breakfast Casseroles

By: Sara Winlet

Copyright © 2012 All rights reserved
No part of this publication may be reproduced in any form or by any means, including scanning, photocopying, or otherwise. Without prior written permission from the copyright holder.

Visit My Other Books

Scrumptious Scones

Scrumptious Muffins

Scrumptious Breakfast Casseroles

Scrumptious Cookies

Scrumptious Pies

Scrumptious Cupcakes

Breakfast Casseroles

Breakfast casseroles are a great way to enjoy a simple and delicious meal your whole family will love. You can easily prep the night before and toss in the oven in the morning, so your family can have a hearty breakfast to start the day. Whether you are looking for a breakfast casserole with hash browns, eggs and sausage or french toast casserole, you will find it, in this tasty breakfast casserole recipe collection.

When I think of breakfast casseroles, it reminds me of a quaint bed and breakfast in North Carolina my husband and I stayed in. The chef prepared a wonderful breakfast casserole that was amazing. So, when I want to relive that wonderful vacation, I make one of these delicious breakfast casseroles.

Table of Contents

SAVORY 4
    Ham and Cheese Hash Brown Casserole 4
    Cheesy Bacon Hash Brown Casserole 5
    Sausage and Cheese Casserole 6
    Country Breakfast Casserole 7
    Spinach and Cheese Breakfast Casserole 8
    Mini Breakfast Casseroles 9
    Maple Sausage Casserole 10
    Sweet and Savory Breakfast Casserole 11
    Cheesy Breakfast Casserole 12
QUICHE 13
    Simple Quiche 13
    Cheesy Chicken Quiche 14
    Bacon Cheddar Quiche 15
    Bacon Asparagus Quiche 16
    Mushroom and Spinach Quiche 17
SWEET 18
    Baked Apple and Raisin French Toast 18
    Baked French Toast 20
    Baked Blueberry French Toast 21
    Baked Cherry French Toast 24
    Peach French Toast Casserole 26
SYRUPS 27
    Simple Strawberry Syrup 27
    Apple Cinnamon Syrup 28
    Cinnamon Cream Syrup 29
    Blueberry Syrup 30

SAVORY

Ham and Cheese Hash Brown Casserole

1 (32oz) package frozen hash brown potatoes
8 eggs
1 cup shredded cheddar cheese
1 pound cooked ham (diced)
2 cups milk
1/2 teaspoon salt

Preheat oven to 350 degrees F.

In a large bowl, combine the hash browns, ham, ½ cup cheese and salt. Spoon into buttered 9x13 baking dish. In another large bowl, whisk eggs and milk then pour over hash brown mixture. Bake for 45-50 minutes until set in the center and knife comes out clean. Sprinkle with remaining half cup of cheese and serve.

Cheesy Bacon Hash Brown Casserole

1 pack of sliced bacon (diced)
1 medium onion (diced)
6 eggs (beaten)
4 cups frozen shredded hash brown potatoes
2 cups shredded sharp cheddar cheese
1 1/4 cups shredded swiss cheese

Preheat oven to 350 degrees F.

In a large skillet, cook bacon and onion until bacon is crisp. Drain bacon and onion place on paper towel and set aside. In a medium bowl, combine eggs, hash brown potatoes, cheddar and swiss cheese, then add bacon mixture. Mix together and pour into a buttered 9x13 inch baking dish. Bake uncovered for 35-40 minutes or until set and bubbly. Let cool for 15 minutes before cutting.

Sausage and Cheese Casserole

2 slices white bread
1/2 pound pork sausage
1/2 cup shredded sharp cheddar cheese
3 eggs
1 cup milk
1/2 teaspoon ground mustard
1/4 teaspoon salt
1/8 teaspoon pepper

Preheat oven to 350 degrees F.

In a skillet, brown the sausage until no longer pink, drain and place on a paper towel to drain off excess grease. Remove the crust from the bread and cut into 1 inch cubes. Place bread in buttered 8 inch baking dish, sprinkle with sausage and cheese. In a medium bowl, whisk the eggs, milk, mustard, salt and pepper. Pour over sausage and cheese. Bake for 30 minutes or until golden brown and set.

Country Breakfast Casserole

6 eggs
2 cups grated sharp cheddar cheese
3 cups plain croutons
1 pack of bacon (about 1 pound)
1 3/4 cups milk
1 bell pepper (diced)
1 tablespoon yellow mustard
salt and pepper to taste

Preheat oven to 325 Degrees F.

Cook bacon in large skillet until browned, crumble and set aside on a paper towel to remove excess grease. Place croutons on the bottom of a buttered 9x13 inch pan. Melt butter and pour over croutons. Sprinkle with cheese.
In a medium bowl mix eggs, milk, peppers, mustard, salt and pepper. Pour mixture over croutons and cheese. Sprinkle with crumbled bacon. Bake for 30 to 40 minutes or until set and lightly brown. Allow to cool for a few minutes before serving.

Spinach and Cheese Breakfast Casserole

(refrigerate overnight)

1 (16 oz) package of spicy pork sausage
4 large eggs
1 block of frozen spinach (thawed, and squeezed dry)
1 can cream of mushroom soup
2 1/4 cups milk
1 cup of fresh mushrooms
1 cup shredded sharp cheddar cheese
1 cup shredded mild white cheese (monterey jack, mozzarella etc.)
1/4 teaspoon dry mustard

In medium skillet cook sausage until no longer pink, place on a paper towel to get off excess grease. Spread croutons on the bottom of a buttered 9x13 inch baking dish. Spread drained sausage over croutons. In a large bowl mix together eggs and milk. Stir in soup, drained spinach, mushrooms, cheese, and mustard. Pour egg mixture over sausage and refrigerate overnight. This will allow the croutons to absorb liquid. The next morning, preheat oven to 350 degrees F. and bake for 50 to 55 minutes or until lightly golden brown and set. Serve hot.

Mini Breakfast Casseroles

1 (12 oz) can of refrigerated regular biscuit dough (not grands)
1/8 cup minced onion
1/8 cup minced bell pepper
3 eggs beaten
3/4 pound breakfast sausage
3 tablespoons milk
1/2 cup shredded colby-monterey jack cheese

Preheat oven to 400 degrees F.

Separate dough into 10 individual biscuits. Flatten each biscuit, then use to line the bottom and sides of 10 greased regular muffin cups. In a large skillet, cook sausage, onions, and green peppers until sausage is evenly brown. Drain on a paper towel to remove excess grease. Evenly distribute drained sausage mixture into biscuit lined muffin cups. In a small bowl mix together eggs and milk. Pour egg mixture evenly in the cups over the sausage mixture. Sprinkle tops with shredded cheese. Bake for 18 to 20 minutes until filling is set.

Maple Sausage Casserole

2 cans butter flake crescent rolls
1 package of maple sausage
2 cups cheddar cheese
9 eggs

Preheat oven to 350 degrees F.

Butter a 9x13 inch baking dish. Line baking dish with one package of crescent rolls. In medium skillet brown sausage, place on paper towel to drain excess grease. In a medium bowl mix eggs and set aside. On top of crescent rolls, layer sausage, shredded cheese, and then pour beaten eggs over the top. Top with second package of crescent rolls. Bake for 35 to 45 minutes or until set in the middle, and lightly browned on top.

Sweet and Savory Breakfast Casserole

2 cups biscuit mix
2 tablespoons sugar
5 medium eggs
1 (16 oz) package of bacon (crisp and crumbled)
3 cups sliced apples
2 cups shredded cheese
2 cups milk

Preheat oven to 375 degrees F.

In medium bowl mix together eggs, milk and biscuit mix, set aside. Mix apples and sugar and layer in a lightly buttered 9x13 inch baking dish. Sprinkle apples with crumbled bacon and shredded cheese. Pour egg mixture evenly over bacon and cheese. Bake for 30-35 minutes or until lightly brown.

Cheesy Breakfast Casserole

1 (16oz) package of hash brown potatoes
1 (16oz) package of pork sausage
1 pound package of Velveeta Cheese (cubed)
8 eggs
1/4 cup milk
salt and pepper to taste

Preheat oven to 350 degrees F.

In a medium skillet brown sausage and place on a paper towel to drain excess
grease. In a medium bowl mix together eggs, milk, salt and pepper, then set aside. In a lightly buttered 9x13 inch baking dish, layer half of the hash browns, half of the sausage, half of the egg mixture and half of the cheese. Repeat layering process with the remaining half of ingredients. Bake for 45 minutes or until center is set.

QUICHE

Simple Quiche

5 eggs (beaten)
1 regular package of bacon
4 oz swiss cheese (grated)
2 tablespoons melted butter
1 1/2 cups milk
1/2 cups all-purpose flour
1 teaspoon salt
1/4 cup onion (diced)
1/4 cup bell pepper (diced)

Preheat oven to 350 degrees F.

Lightly butter a 9 inch pie pan and set aside. In a medium skillet cook bacon until evenly brown, drain on paper towel, crumble and set aside. Line bottom of pie plate with cheese and bacon. In a medium bowl, whisk eggs, butter, onion, bell pepper, salt, flour, and milk. Pour mixture over cheese and bacon. Bake for 35 minutes or until set in the middle

Cheesy Chicken Quiche

1 (9 inch) deep dish unbaked pie shell
1/2 cup of frozen spinach(drained and squeezed dry)
1 cup cheddar cheese (shredded)
1 cup chicken (cooked and diced)
4 eggs
1/2 cup milk
1/8 teaspoon black pepper
1/4 teaspoon salt
3/4 cup mayonnaise (not miracle whip)
1/4 cup onion (diced)

Preheat oven to 350 degrees F.

Press ¼ cup of cheese into bottom of unbaked pie crust. Combine chicken, spinach, onion, and remaining cheese, and place in pie shell. In a medium bowl, mix eggs, milk, mayonnaise, salt and pepper. Pour evenly over spinach mixture. Bake for 40-45 minutes or until set in the middle. Let cool 10- 15 minutes before cutting.

Bacon Cheddar Quiche

1/2 cup biscuit mix
1 1/2 cups milk
4 eggs
8 strips of bacon
3/4 cups cheddar cheese (shredded)
1/4 teaspoon pepper
1/2 cups butter (melted)

Preheat oven to 350 degrees F.

In a medium skillet cook bacon until crisp, place bacon on a paper towel, crumble and set aside. In a large bowl, whisk eggs, milk, and butter, add in biscuit mix, pepper and mix well. Pour into a deep dish 9 inch pie plate. Top with crumbled bacon and cheese. Bake for 30-35 minutes or until middle is set. Let cool for 10 minutes before cutting.

Bacon Asparagus Quiche

1 pack of bacon
1 pound fresh asparagus (trimmed)
1 (9 inch) deep dish unbaked pie shell
1 cup swiss cheese (shredded)
3 eggs
1/2 cup half-and-half cream
1/4 teaspoon pepper
1/4 teaspoon salt
1/2 cup onion (diced)
1 tablespoon all-purpose flour

Preheat oven to 400 degrees F.

In a medium skillet cook, bacon adding onions at the end to saute. Drain bacon and onions and place on a paper towel to drain excess grease. Cut 8 asparagus spears into 4 inch long spears for top of quiche. Cut the remaining asparagus into 1 inch pieces and boil until tender then drain. In a small bowl, combine eggs, and cream and set aside. In a medium bowl, mix together bacon, onion, asparagus pieces, cheese, flour, salt, and pepper. Place mixture into pie shell and pour egg mixture over the top. Place asparagus spears in a pattern on top of quiche, then bake for 30-35 minutes until quiche is set in the middle. Let cool for 10 minutes before cutting.

Mushroom and Spinach Quiche

1 (9 inch) unbaked deep dish pie crust
1 pound pork sausage
1 pound fresh mushrooms (sliced)
3 eggs
1 cup half-and-half cream
1/4 teaspoon salt
1/2 cup grated parmesan cheese

Preheat oven to 400 degrees F.

In a medium skillet, cook sausage until brown adding the mushrooms at the end to saute. Drain sausage and mushrooms with a slotted spoon, and place onto a paper towel to drain excess grease. In a large bowl, whisk eggs, cream, cheese and salt. Add sausage and mushrooms to egg mixture and mix well. Pour mixture into unbaked pie shell. Bake for 25 to 30 minutes or until middle is set. Let cool for 10 minutes before slicing.

SWEET

Baked Apple and Raisin French Toast
(refrigerate overnight)

3 apples (peeled, cored and sliced)
1 (1 pound) french loaf baguette, cut into 1 inch cubes
1/2 cup butter, melted
1 cup brown sugar
1 teaspoon ground cinnamon
1/2 cup raisins
6 eggs beaten
1 1/2 cups milk
1 tablespoon vanilla extract
2 teaspoon ground cinnamon

Butter a 9x13 inch baking dish. In a large bowl mix sliced apples, raisins brown sugar, melted butter and 1 teaspoon of cinnamon, coat evenly. Pour into prepared baking dish. Arrange bread slices in an even layer over apples. In a bowl mix together eggs, milk, vanilla, and 2 teaspoon of cinnamon. Pour over bread making sure every slice is fully soaked. Cover with aluminum foil and refrigerate over night. Bake covered in a preheated 375 degree F. for 40 to 45 minutes. Let stand for 5 minutes before serving. Top with your favorite pancake syrup.

Baked French Toast

4 eggs
5 cups cubed bread
3 tablespoons sugar (divided)
1/4 teaspoon salt
1 teaspoon vanilla extract
1 tablespoon butter (softened)
1 teaspoon ground cinnamon

Preheat oven to 350 degrees F.

Lightly butter an 8x8 inch baking dish. In a medium bowl, mix eggs, milk, 2 tablespoons sugar, salt and vanilla then set aside. Line bottom of pan with bread cubes. Pour egg mixture over bread cubes, then dot with butter. In a small bowl, mix together 2 tablespoons of sugar and 1 tablespoon of cinnamon sprinkle over the top. Bake for 45 to 50 minutes, until golden brown. Top with your favorite syrup.

Baked Blueberry French Toast

(refrigerate overnight)

12 eggs (beaten)
2 cups milk
12 slices of day old bread (cube)
2 (8oz) packages of cream cheese (cut into cubes)
1 teaspoon vanilla extract
1/3 cup maple syrup
1 cup sugar
2 tablespoons cornstarch
1 cup water
2 cup fresh or frozen blueberries (divided)
1 tablespoon butter

In a large bowl mix eggs, milk, vanilla extract, and syrup then set aside. In a lightly butter a 9x13 inch baking dish, arrange half of bread cubes and top with cream cheese cubes. Sprinkle 1 cup of blueberries on top of cream cheese then top with remaining bread crumbs. Pour egg mixture over bread crumbs, cover and refrigerate overnight. In the morning take french toast out of refrigerator and allow to warm for 30 minutes. Preheat oven to 350 degrees F. Bake covered 30 minutes then remove cover for 25-30 minutes until center is firm and surface is lightly brown.

For topping: In a medium sauce pan mix sugar, cornstarch, water, and blueberries and bring to a boil. Boil for 3-4 minutes stirring constantly. Reduce heat and simmer for 10 minutes. Stir in the 1 tablespoon of butter and pour over baked french toast.

Baked Strawberry Banana French Toast

4 individual ramekins (or small baking dishes)
4 slices of cubed bread (crustless)
1 banana (smashed)
1 cup diced strawberries
3 eggs (beaten)
1/2 cup milk
1/4 teaspoon cinnamon
1 1/2 teaspoon vanilla extract
maple syrup for serving

Preheat oven to 375 degrees F.

In a medium bowl, mix smashed banana, strawberries, milk, eggs, cinnamon and vanilla, then set aside. Butter individual ramekins or small baking dish. Place bread cubes in dishes, then pour milk mixture over bread cubes and gently toss to coat. Bake 20-25 minutes or until set in the middle. Serve with maple syrup or your favorite pancake syrup.

Baked Cherry French Toast

(Refrigerate Overnight)

1/2 loaf of French bread (sliced)
1 loaf of white bread (diced)
7 eggs (beaten)
4 cups frozen cherries (drained)
1 1/2 cups milk
1 1/2 cups half and half
2 teaspoons vanilla extract
1/2 teaspoon nutmeg
1/2 teaspoon cinnamon
1/2 cup sugar

topping:
½ cup butter (melted)
1 cup packed brown sugar
2 tablespoons of dark corn syrup
1 cup chopped nuts (walnuts or pecans)

In a medium bowl, mix eggs, milk, half and half, vanilla, nutmeg, cinnamon and sugar then set aside. Place cubed loaf of white bread in the bottom of a buttered 9x13 inch baking dish. Spread the cherries over the bread. Arrange sliced french bread over the top of the cherries. Pour egg mixture over the french bread slices. Combine melted butter, corn syrup, brown sugar, and nuts then spread over the bread.

Cover and refrigerate overnight. The next morning preheat oven to 350 degrees F. Bake for 45-50 minutes or until set in the middle and lightly golden brown on top.

Peach French Toast Casserole

(Refrigerate overnight)

12 slices of day old French bread (3/4 inch thick)
5 eggs (beaten)
1 cup packed brown sugar
1/2 cup butter
2 tablespoons water
1 (29 oz) can of sliced peaches, drained
1 tablespoon vanilla extract
1 teaspoon ground cinnamon (to taste)

In a saucepan, bring to a boil brown sugar, butter and water stir frequently. Reduce heat and simmer for 10 minutes. Cover the bottom of a 9x13 inch baking dish with the brown sugar mixture. Layer drained peaches over the brown sugar mixture then top with slices of the French bread. In a medium bowl mix eggs and vanilla. Pour egg mixture over the French bread making sure to soak the bread evenly. Sprinkle cinnamon on top cover and refrigerate overnight. The next morning, remove the dish from the refrigerator and allow to warm for 30 minutes. Preheat oven to 350 degrees F. Bake for 25-30 minutes until set in middle and lightly golden brown on top.

SYRUPS

Tip: Double syrup recipes for more servings

Simple Strawberry Syrup

1 cup sugar
1 cup water
1 1/2 cups smashed strawberries

In a medium sauce pan bring sugar, and water to a boil. Add in strawberries and return to a boil, then simmer uncovered for 10 minutes, stirring occasionally. Serve immediately over pancakes or waffles, refrigerate any unused syrup.

Apple Cinnamon Syrup

2 tart apples (diced)
1/2 cup sugar
1 tablespoon ground cinnamon
2 tablespoons water

In a medium sauce pan combine apples, sugar, cinnamon, and water. Mix well and bring to a boil. Reduce heat and simmer for 10 minutes until apples are tender and sauce is thickened. Refrigerate any unused syrup.

Cinnamon Cream Syrup

1 cup sugar
1/2 cup light corn syrup
1/4 cup water
3/4 teaspoon ground cinnamon
1/2 cup heavy whipping cream

In a medium sauce pan mix sugar, corn syrup, water, and cinnamon bring to a boil. Boil for 2 minutes stirring constantly. Remove from heat cool for 5 minutes then stir in cream. Serve over pancakes or french toast. Refrigerate any unused syrup.

Blueberry Syrup

1 cup blueberries
1/4 cup sugar
1/4 cup water

In a medium saucepan combine blueberries, sugar and water. Bring to a boil, crush blueberries and simmer for 2-3 minutes until slightly thickened. Serve over pancakes. Refrigerate any unused syrup.

John 3:16 For God so loved the world, that he gave his only begotten Son, that whosoever believeth in him should not perish, but have everlasting life.

Made in the USA
Middletown, DE
10 February 2016